Take
Time
for
You

Take Time for You

A book to inspire happy, healthy, stress-free living for women

Mary Butler
and
Diane Mastromarino

Blue Mountain Press™
Boulder, Colorado

Library of Congress Catalog Card Number: 2006030261
ISBN: 978-1-59842-193-4

▐ and Blue Mountain Press are registered in U.S. Patent and Trademark Office.
Certain trademarks are used under license.

ACKNOWLEDGMENTS appear on page 96.

Printed in China.
First Printing: 2007

✪ This book is printed on recycled paper.

This book is printed on fine quality, laid embossed, 80 lb. paper. This paper has been specially produced to be acid free (neutral pH) and contains no groundwood or unbleached pulp. It conforms with all the requirements of the American National Standards Institute, Inc., so as to ensure that this book will last and be enjoyed by future generations.

Library of Congress Cataloging-in-Publication Data

Butler, Mary, 1974-
    Take time for you : a book to inspire happy, healthy, stress-free living for women / Mary Butler and Diane Mastromarino.
        p. cm.
    ISBN: 978-1-59842-193-4 (trade pbk. : alk. paper)
    1. Women—Life skills guides 2. Women—Conduct of life.
I. Mastromarino, Diane, 1978- II. Title.

    HQ1221.B955 2006
    158.082—dc22

                                                    2006030261

Blue Mountain Arts, Inc.
P.O. Box 4549, Boulder, Colorado 80306

Contents

Get to know yourself
Find out what is important to you
Find out what you are good at
Give yourself freedom to try out new things
Take part in the beauty of nature
Live life to the fullest
Create your own dreams

— Susan Polis Schutz

Introduction

Imagine how incredible it would be to pencil a little time for yourself into your daily schedule. Don't worry, you don't have to uproot your current lifestyle or pull away from the people who depend on you most. Taking time for yourself can be as simple as slowing down a little bit... sleeping in when your body cries out for more rest... spending quality time with girlfriends you haven't seen in a while... soaking in a tub scented with lavender and chamomile... eating foods that nourish your body and energize your spirit... and painting your nails red and your walls a golden yellow hue.

This book is about recognizing people like you who work so hard and give so much of themselves to others. It's to remind you that in order to take care of the people in your life, sometimes it's best for everyone if you put your needs first.

There's joy to be found in everything you do. You can nourish your spirit, your mind, and your body every day. Begin your journey with a smile... and start taking steps toward the happy, healthy, stress-free life you deserve.

HAPPY

Every morning, wake with the awe
of just being alive.
Each day, discover the magnificent,
awesome beauty in the world.
Explore and embrace life in yourself
and in everything you see.
Live every day well.
Let a little sunshine out as well as in.
Create your own rainbows.
Be open to possibilities.
Believe in miracles!

— Vickie M. Worsham

Create a "You Spot"

No matter how many children, roommates, dogs, or monsters under the bed you have residing in your home, you deserve a "you spot," a place you can escape to and leave the rest of your world behind.

This "you spot" can be an office, a den, a small corner by the window, a quiet nook in your garden, or any other place that you can be completely by yourself. Designate this spot as yours, and make sure everyone in your home is aware of it, even Fido or Whiskers. This is the place you will come to clear your mind. Keep a journal and some markers or crayons in your spot for creative moments. Meditate, stretch, lounge — whatever makes you feel happiest. Think of time spent in this place as a time to unwind, a time to shed the day's frustrations and stress... a time just for you.

You must have a room, or a certain hour or so a day, where you don't know what was in the newspapers that morning, you don't know who your friends are, you don't know what you owe anybody, you don't know what anybody owes to you. This is a place where you can simply experience and bring forth what you are and what you might be.

— Joseph Campbell

❧ No phones allowed. No one, no matter who they are or where they are calling from, is allowed to invade your space. They can leave a message and you can get back to them when you feel refreshed.

❧ It doesn't matter if you have a big exam, a huge deadline, or housework that needs to be done. You will be able to tackle it more efficiently if you give your mind a little downtime to unwind.

❧ This is not a time to balance your checkbook, clean out your purse, or pay the bills. Nor is it a time to organize your day planner or make a to-do list.

❧ Though they may be the angels on your earth or the stars in your sky, your children are not welcome into your sacred place. If they are old enough, use this as a learning experience for them to explore their own quiet time.

❧ They're cute and furry, yes, and sometimes even great stress-busters, but pets can be a distraction. They need attention, and this is a time for your attention to be focused solely on you.

❧ The most important thing to remember is this: stress of any kind is not allowed to creep into your "you spot."

Bring Nature Indoors

We have all experienced the joyous feeling of coming home to the beauty of fresh flowers on the kitchen table, the excitement when a plant we've cared for sprouts a new leaf, or the refreshing smell of herbs ready to be picked to spice up a meal. We have an unspoken tie with the natural world; the way it affects our emotions and our senses is a truly wonderful gift.

Bringing flowers, plants, and herb gardens inside is not only a great way to brighten the atmosphere, but it can add an element of life to your home. Caring for another living thing is truly revitalizing for the human soul. Whether it is providing water, sunlight, touch, or quiet conversation, tending to the needs of plant life helps to shift your focus outward, away from the worrisome pressure the day brings. It cultivates a sense of satisfaction and accomplishment knowing that you are responsible for the growth of something beautiful and alive.

It is simply gratifying to nurture something, to tend to something that responds so readily to our care. Who can fail to marvel at the ability of a tiny seed to sprout and grow and present us with lustrous blooms, tasty salad fixings, or a canopy of shade?

— Karen York

With Fresh Flowers

- Cut plant stems at an angle to help increase water absorption and re-cut the stems a little bit every two days.
- Place flowers in warm water with fresh floral food to make blooms last longer.
- Remove leaves that are below the waterline to prevent bacterial growth.
- Keep your flowers in a cool spot away from direct sunlight, drafts from fans or air conditioners, and the tops of televisions or radiators.

With Plants

- Evenly water entire soil surface until just a little water drains out the bottom of the pot.
- In the wintertime, reduce watering and feeding so the plant can rest.
- Repot plants when they have grown too large for their current pot or you can see the roots coming through the bottom hole of the pot.

With Herbs

- Herbs should receive at least four hours of sunlight daily.
- Use soil with low to medium fertility.
- Clip and use cuttings regularly to keep plants' shape.
- Keep in warmer temperatures unless otherwise directed.

Live in Color

Think of your favorite color. Think of how it makes you feel. If it's yellow, does it make you feel joyful when you see a bouquet of sunflowers? If it's blue, does watching the sky calm you? Color can have a great effect on your mood, stress level, and performance. Color therapy extends beyond thinking about your favorite color. Each color promotes a series of emotions and attitudes. Paying special attention to the colors that surround you is a simple way to improve mood, productivity, and overall well-being.

Be creative. Paint your bedroom walls or put colored draperies on the windows. Too drastic for you? Start simply by hanging a poster, changing the screen saver on your computer, or buying a small area rug. If you've been feeling a little down, choose uplifting, happy colors. Overwhelmed or stressed? Choose colors that promote calmness and serenity. You may even notice your color choices affecting the people around you.

Let color in and she will show you her riches. Just as a bright lipstick, a shawl, and pretty earrings can open a wardrobe to beauty, colorful fabrics, walls, and accessories can do the same for your surroundings.

— April Cornell

Red is... the color of passion and of strength, motivation, and physical drive. It... fills us with the energy to get things done.

> **Color Tip:** Buy a red clock to stimulate productivity.

 Yellow... is connected to matters of the intellect and detachment, and induces a rational, discerning approach linked to mental control.... Yellow... is an expansive and optimistic color, one that is light, pure, positive, and uplifting in nature.

> **Color Tip:** To promote mental growth, write notes on a yellow pad.

 Green is the color associated with balance and harmony.... It is the color of kindness, compassion, caring, and sharing. Green is comforting and stress-relieving.

> **Color Tip:** Throw a green area rug on the floor to promote balance and stability.

 Blue is the color for calm.... Blue is cooling, pacifying, and comforting, and it helps us to wind down, adopt a more leisurely pace, and simply relax.

> **Color Tip:** Paint your door blue so that you can begin your evening leaving behind stress and embracing true calmness.

> — Catherine Cumming

Be an Artist

As a child, you probably finger-painted, colored outside the lines, and ate more paste than was healthy. Making art is part of growing up. Teachers, parents, and other adults encourage children to express themselves through color, texture, and shapes. But these creative activities tend to fall by the wayside with age.

If you're like most adults, you moved on with your education and life and forgot about how fun it is to paint, make pottery, or weave simple textiles. You may not be able to draw a straight line to save your life. So what? When you pick up a paintbrush or stick your hands in wet clay, you'll be doing it to have fun, to relieve stress, or to express a creative side that doesn't get a lot of use.

The woman who needs to create works of art is born with a kind of psychic tension in her which drives her unmercifully to find a way to balance, to make herself whole. Every human being has this need: in the artist it is mandatory.

— May Sarton

Express Yourself

- Paint a landscape.
- Hook a rug.
- Learn to knit.
- Take a pottery class.
- Collect seashells and use them to make mosaics, sculptures, or jewelry.
- Study photography.
- Make a quilt from old blue jeans.
- Refinish a piece of furniture.
- Scrapbook.
- Carve something from a piece of wood.
- Create origami.
- Make a collage.

Tell Your Story

One of the most freeing escapes from everyday life is the practice of writing. It provides an opportunity to look within yourself for inspiration, to open your mind, and to let the words spill forth from your memory and your imagination. The point is to express your thoughts and experiences in any form that fits: poems, plays, limericks, essays, songs, a diary, screenplay, blog, or novel.

A writer's mantra is write what you know. So when you sit down to begin, give yourself an assignment: ten minutes on where you grew up or something you can describe in great detail. If you're passionate about the topic, that's even better. Get excited, ignite your mind, and let your hand (or your fingers) fly. Don't stop until your time is up. Forget about proper language use and spelling. Just do it. You'll be amazed at how light your head and body feel after you're done.

When you write, don't say, "I'm going to write a poem." That attitude will freeze you right away. Sit down with the least expectation of yourself; say, "I am free to write the worst junk in the world."

— Natalie Goldberg

Write It Down

- 🌿 Write at the same time every day. Put aside a set amount of time every day or several days a week — say thirty minutes every Monday, Wednesday, and Friday.

- 🌿 Choose a topic, set a timer, and keep writing until your time's up. Called "freewriting," this five- to ten-minute exercise helps ignite your creativity and can jump-start every writing session.

- 🌿 Forget about the rules: grammar, punctuation, spelling, and getting the facts straight.

- 🌿 Role-play and write from different points of view.

- 🌿 Fully develop and describe the movie in your mind. Instead of "the young girl," zero in on the details: "the ten-year-old with brown braided pigtails wearing a pink fairy costume." Not "a red car," but "a dirty, red late-model station wagon with missing hubcaps."

- 🌿 Join a writer's group. In just about every city, there are groups for writers of all genres, from people who write bodice-ripping romance stories to those who pen true-crime tales. Hobbyists and beginners as well as published writers often join these groups as a way to garner feedback and enjoy the support and encouragement of others.

Celebrate Half-Birthdays

Birthdays can be wonderful: the cake, the attention, the cards and gifts. The trouble with them is that there's no way to escape the pressure of that bigger number that tells the world just how grown up you really are — or should be. You've hit another milestone, and you can't help but pick apart your life's resume... you still haven't lost those ten pounds, been promoted at work, or taken your dream vacation.

This year, create a new tradition: observe your half-birthday. As a kid, maybe you didn't celebrate it, but you most likely told people when you were 5½, 8½, and 12½. The beauty of adulthood is you make your own rules.

You can treat the day as a time of reflection... or take the day to pamper yourself with a manicure, a massage, or a trip to the lingerie department. Who doesn't need a new leopard-print bra on her 35½ birthday?

Most of us have been trained to continually strive for the next thing, and the next, and the next. However, if we deprive ourselves of happiness along the way, if we convince ourselves that joy exists only at our desired destination, we become caught in an endless cycle of wanting and waiting, and waiting and wanting.

— Debbie Ford

Fun with Fractions

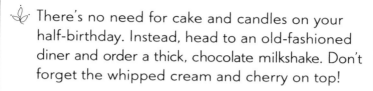 There's no need for cake and candles on your half-birthday. Instead, head to an old-fashioned diner and order a thick, chocolate milkshake. Don't forget the whipped cream and cherry on top!

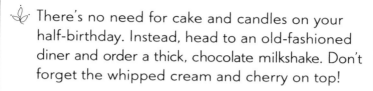 Work a half-day.

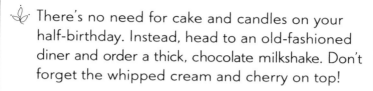 Cut your daily visit to the gym in half, and spend the remainder of the time soaking in a hot tub, steaming in the sauna, or getting a massage.

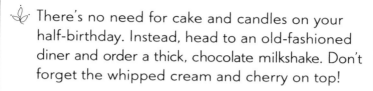 Get there half as fast. Ride your bike, walk, or simply take your time traveling to the day's destinations.

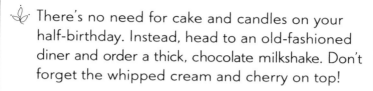 Dig up a half-as-old photo of yourself and carry it in your wallet for the day as a reminder of what you were like at that time in your life. If you're feeling daring, e-mail or call a long-lost friend from that period in your life.

 Wear a miniskirt and pair it with ½-inch, 1½-inch, 2½-inch, or another fractional-height pair of heels.

Go Solo

There's a rock show that sounds like fun... you've always wanted to check out a particular art museum... a wine-tasting class is being offered at a local restaurant... but you can't find anyone to go with you. Instead of shrugging off your curiosity, pencil in a date with yourself on your calendar.

Granted, going solo can be a scary concept. But sometimes you just need to forget about what everybody else wants to do and muster your courage to explore the unknown. You might find that you're not destined to be a wine connoisseur or a white-water kayaker, but why not entertain the possibilities?

Treat your outing like a special adventure. Chances are, stepping out of your comfort zone will make you grow as a person and enhance your life. You might make a new friend or two and discover that sometimes you only need yourself to have a good time.

Solitude is taking pride in knowing that you are able to amuse yourself, take care of yourself, or being deliciously lost in your own thoughts.

— Sasha Cagen

Embrace Solitude

- Go to a movie alone.
- Bake bread.
- Have coffee in a coffee shop.
- Read in the park.
- Check out a new artist, musician, venue.
- Cook.
- People-watch.
- Write letters.
- Travel on your own.
- Explore a new part of town.
- Spend hours by the ocean.
- Lie on the couch with a good book.
- Organize/file.
- Rent a movie only you want to see.
- Exercise.
- Dance around your house.
- Sing in the mirror.
- Fly a kite.
- Take a long walk.

Nurture Your Spiritual Self

Just about everyone on this planet, at one time or another, has asked herself: What is this life all about? What do all the happy, sad, and in-between moments add up to? While you may never truly know the meaning of life, it is possible to answer another very important question: What is the purpose of *your* life? You, of course, are the only one who can solve this very important mystery.

For many people, one of the first steps to discovering your place in the world is to look inward and focus on your spiritual beliefs. What is it that you feel strongly about? What makes you passionate? What are the things that make you feel fulfilled? What are you unsure about? What are your beliefs?

How are you fulfilling your spiritual needs now? If you find yourself wanting to do more to better yourself... to help others... to understand the universe beyond yourself, it might be time to explore how to best nourish your soul.

This soul, or life within us, by no means agrees with the life outside us. If one has the courage to ask her what she thinks, she is always saying the very opposite to what other people say.

— Virginia Woolf

Have Faith

Learn
- Join a spiritual study group.
- Read a historical book about your faith.

Act
- Volunteer to help with spiritual services at your church, synagogue, mosque or meditation center.
- Join a yoga studio.
- Take a religious retreat.
- Walk a labyrinth.

Explore
- Shop for a house of worship that suits your style. Feel free to try out different services to find the right fit. Lists of services of all types can be found in the religion section of your local newspaper.

Give of Yourself

Taking time for yourself can also mean feeding that part of you that wants to give back to others and sharing your gifts. Helping others feels good, no doubt about it. Consider what it might be like to teach adults to read, walk dogs at the Humane Society, feed fox kits and fledgling birds at a wildlife rehabilitation sanctuary, or volunteer to play games with hospitalized children.

Make your contribution one day a week or a few hours a month. The important thing is to do something that interests you and makes you proud. Just think of how your life might be bettered by giving one afternoon twelve times a year to a worthy cause.

Making a difference in your community might mean taking an elderly neighbor out to lunch or running errands that require extra hands, helping out at your neighborhood school's annual bake sale, or cheering up a friend who's been going through a hard time. You can make it anything you want... just never forget that you have something to give.

Sometimes when we are generous in small, barely detectable ways it can change someone else's life forever.

— Margaret Cho

Give Back to Your Community — and Beyond

In Your Community

- Tutor children as part of an after-school program.
- Help out at an adult day care.
- Adopt a stretch of highway and pick up litter once a month.
- Paint a neighborhood mural.
- Support a political cause.
- Adopt a road median and plant colorful flowers.
- Donate blood.
- Find other opportunities online, in your local newspaper, or ask your friends where they volunteer.

Beyond

- Take a "volunteer vacation"! Use your skills and interests in areas of the world where help is needed.
- Your church or synagogue may organize volunteer service projects in other parts of the country and the world.
- Contact an area hospital to see if you can help with an upcoming "medical mission" to another part of the world, or organize a drive for medical supplies and then arrange for shipping them to their intended destination.
- Host an international student through your local school district or an area college or university.

Embrace Friendship

So many times when life gets stressful and the days become hectic, the first thing most of us do is lose all contact with the outside world. We tend to push people away during these trying times to gain control of all the other things we are juggling. There just aren't enough hours in the day for everything, and socializing, most times, finds its way to the bottom of our priority list when, really, it should be at the very top.

Friends are your support system. They are the ones who truly care what you are going through and want to be there to help you. In hectic times, welcome friendship to hold your hand, help you breathe, provide sane advice, and keep you steady on your feet.

Friends are like home. They're that place we can come to relax, put up our feet, have some fun, and find relief from the rest of the world.

— Noelle Cleary and Dini von Mueffling

Make Time for Friends

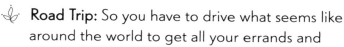 **Road Trip:** So you have to drive what seems like around the world to get all your errands and tasks accomplished. Pick up your friend on the way. Crank up the tunes and fill each other in on what you've been missing.

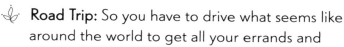 **Late Night:** Call your friend during the day and tell her to keep her phone by her bed that night along with a warm cup of cocoa. Plan a phone date to unwind from the day. It's nice to get everything off your chest before floating off into dreamland.

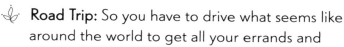 **Anytime Letter:** Sometimes meeting up or finding the right moment for a phone call is just not possible. Instead of doodling between work assignments or writing in your journal, pen a letter to a friend to let her know you haven't forgotten about her.

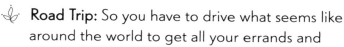 **Gym Talk:** Exercise can be a lot more enjoyable if you pair it with your favorite friend. Climb on the stairclimber side by side or go for a run in the park on your lunch breaks. This is a great way to combine exercise and friendship and doubly reduce the day's tension and stress.

Savor Your Successes

You completed a big project, ran your first 10K, or got the raise you've been asking for. Maybe you did something smaller, like resisted that slice of chocolate cake at your friend's birthday party or made it to the gym three days this week, and now you can't help but smile when you step on the scale. Give yourself a toast.

Take your time getting ready in the morning. Wear an outfit you love. Post a reminder of your accomplishment or a note of congratulations to yourself in a place where you'll see it throughout the day. Even better: send yourself a bouquet of your favorite flowers.

Remember there are benefits to patting yourself on the back every now and again. You'll be invigorated and reminded of why you work so hard in the first place — and before you know it, you'll be ready to acknowledge your everyday achievements again.

When you do something wonderful, take time out of your day to not only acknowledge yourself, but do something nice for yourself.... If you treat each day and each event as just part of the job or one of many responsibilities, all days begin to look the same.

— Jeff Davidson

Applaud Yourself...

- Wear a flower in your hair.

- Slip $20 into the pocket of a piece of clothing to be found as a surprise later on. Depending on the season — if it's summer, use your winter coat, or if it's winter, your favorite shorts.

- Write "Good job!" on a sticky note and attach it to the side of your computer monitor along with all your other "notes to self."

- Smile at yourself when you look in the mirror, and not just so you can check whether there's food in your teeth. If you need a reminder to smile, write one... in bright-red lipstick.

- Toast yourself at the dinner table, even if you're just washing down pizza or leftovers with diet soda. Invite some friends over to share the fun. Use your best glasses — crystal, if you have them.

HEALTHY

If we treat our bodies properly by giving them healthy food and the right amount of physical activity, they will return the favor. They will pay us back with energy, vitality, a clear mind, and a clean bill of health.

— Martina Navratilova

Stressercise

When you think exercise, your body may quiver, anticipating things like sweat, burn, hard work, and exhaustion. Though your body isn't completely wrong in recognizing exercise's ability to be physically draining, exercise can have the opposite effect mentally.

Exercise releases endorphins, which induce feelings of well-being and relaxation. Endorphins have been said to actually decrease stress and pain, as well as increase memory and brain power. By making exercise a normal part of your weekly routine, your endorphins continue to flow, creating a healthy cycle for your body. This in turn keeps you feeling energized and happy all day long. Taking exercise classes, playing sports, or working out with a friend puts your mind's focus on something else and allows a break from stress and tension. Solitary exercising, like long runs or bike rides, allows time for you to work through thoughts and feelings and search for answers and solutions. Figure out which type of exercise works best for you, and get your body moving.

I find the best antidote for worry is exercise. Use your muscles more and your brain less when you are worried, and you will be surprised at the results.

— Dale Carnegie

Move Your Body

- 🌿 Do sit-ups while waiting for the coffee to brew.
- 🌿 Carry groceries into the house one bag at a time.
- 🌿 Jump rope.
- 🌿 Ride your bike or walk to work.
- 🌿 Go out dancing with your friends.
- 🌿 Get up to change the channel on the TV instead of using the remote control.
- 🌿 Take the stairs instead of the elevator.
- 🌿 Walk the dog.
- 🌿 Park your car in the space farthest from your destination.
- 🌿 Carry a bunch of boxes for a friend who's moving.

- 🌿 Do yoga while watching TV.
- 🌿 Go to the park and climb on the monkey bars.
- 🌿 Rearrange the furniture in your house.
- 🌿 Shovel snow or rake leaves.

Cleanse Your Temple

In alternative medicine, a spring housecleaning applies quite literally to the place you really live: your body. Many people make it an annual practice to "cleanse" or "detox" themselves of the toxins they inhale in the air or consume unknowingly in food, drinks, and even prescription medications. When alcohol, tobacco, pesticides, and heavy metals filter through your system, residual amounts are left behind. A cleanse supplements what the liver already does, but many people believe in a detox's ability to boost energy, clear the skin, and provide greater mental clarity.

A simple approach involves setting aside one full day. The night before, eat a light meal. Avoid caffeine, tobacco, and alcohol. Go to bed early and allow yourself to awake naturally in the morning. Begin the next day with a steaming hot shower or bath.

Drink hot water with lemon instead of soft drinks, coffee, or tea. Your meals ought to be natural, low in calories, and high in fiber. Many people begin with a juice fast.

Because time is the one thing most of us don't have enough of, we cut corners. We eat convenience or junk food, we don't get enough sleep, we can't fit in exercise, and we often drink too much or smoke as a quick-fix way to relax. Deep down, we all know this is no way to live.

— Anna Selby

The Fruit and Vegetable Fast

- **Breakfast:** Natural yogurt with seeds. Apple and carrot juice.
- **Mid-morning:** Apple.
- **Lunch:** As much salad as you like made from any of the following raw ingredients: bean sprouts, beetroot, broccoli, carrots, celery, chicory, cucumber, peppers, radishes, spring onions, watercress, and any kind of salad leaves. Dress with a little yogurt and black pepper. Any vegetable juice.
- **Mid-afternoon:** Apple.
- **Supper:** As much fruit salad as you like, made with fresh fruit and a little orange or apple juice to sweeten. Again, you can have a couple of spoonfuls of natural yogurt with this. Choose a fruit juice.

Drink plenty of herb teas and water throughout the day — aim for around 48 ounces at least.

— Anna Selby

Create a New Food Attitude

When life gets busy, we push ourselves the hardest and expect the most from our minds and bodies. In the midst of our craziness, good nutrition quickly falls to the bottom of our priority list.

It's true that there won't always be time for an eight-course meal or a colorful plate of food, but that doesn't mean your body should run on empty... or on empty calories. Satisfying hunger with fast-food meals or vending machine goodies will not provide the energy you need to make it through your hectic day. Think back to the food pyramid you learned about in second grade, the one that seemed to be a magnificent ploy to get you to eat your vegetables. Good nutrition is just as important now as it was back then. As an adult who's always on the go, you need your nutrients and vitamins more than ever. A well-balanced diet is essential to your well-being. Food is fuel, and eating healthy should always remain on the top of your to-do list.

Many people ignore the profound effects that food can have on mood, intellect, and energy level. In fact, not eating right will affect your memory, mood, and vitality long before it will affect your heart and bones.

— Elizabeth Somer, MA, RD

Eat for Health

- Eat a breakfast that includes some protein and some carbohydrates.
- Limit caffeinated beverages to three servings per day or fewer, and don't drink tea or coffee with meals.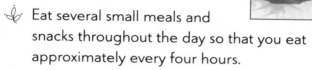
- Eat several small meals and snacks throughout the day so that you eat approximately every four hours.
- If you crave carbohydrates, plan a carbohydrate-rich snack for your low-energy period of the day.
- Do not overeat in the evening and avoid excessive snacking after dinner.
- Consume ample amounts of iron-rich foods.
- Avoid severe calorie-restricted diets. Too few calories means too little fuel and nutrients, which can leave you drowsy.
- Drink water.
- Avoid alcohol consumption or limit your intake to no more than five drinks a week.

— Elizabeth Somer, MA, RD

Kick a Bad Habit

So you've got a bad habit — just about everybody does. One of the best things you can do for yourself is to kick it. Erase it from your days. Move past this phase in your life and learn from it. You might be a chronic procrastinator or a smoker, a binge drinker or a nail biter. Breaking any ingrained behavior is tough to do. But if a habit makes you feel bad about yourself, stresses you out, or has the potential to make you sick, it's in your best interest to take the time and make the effort to stop doing it... right now.

You wouldn't want other people to treat you the way you sometimes do. Respect your mind, body, and soul. Find a way to stop doing the things that you know you shouldn't do. Once you're free of this nagging problem, you'll feel so much better when you wake up in the morning... when you look in the mirror... and when you think about how others perceive you. Be the beautiful person you know you are.

Habits are often formed because we use the behavior as some kind of reward. But eventually, changing that behavior can make us feel better than the habit ever could — it's a far better reward, and the self-esteem and confidence that ensue are tremendous.

— Cherry Pedrick

Ditch Your Crutches

- Decide how serious you are about breaking the bad habit. Are you willing to devote the time and energy necessary to stop it once and for all?
- Carry a small journal and write down when and where you engage in the behavior you'd like to quit. Also note how you feel and what you're doing at the moment.
- Consider what the habit does for you. Do you use it as a way to deal with stress, anxiety, boredom, fear, or anger?
- Think of healthy, positive alternatives to the behavior, and practice them to see what works best. If you're trying to stop yelling at your kids (or others) when you're angry, you might try walking away — into another room or just a few feet away — to cool off instead. If that's not working, maybe drink a glass of water.
- Ask for help from those around you. Tell them your goal and what they can do to help you achieve it.
- Most importantly, be positive. Don't beat yourself up if you have bad days. Be patient with yourself.

Take a Deep Breath

There's a good reason people always advise "take a deep breath" when you're upset or nervous. Deep breathing is calming. It releases tension. Because you have to think about doing it, deep breathing forces you to focus on the moment.

For centuries, practitioners of yoga have known how deep breathing can immediately improve the way you feel. Besides helping to relax the body, yogic breathing infuses your blood with oxygen, boosting your energy.

Try the following exercise:

- Find a quiet spot where you can sit comfortably in a chair or cross-legged on the floor.
- Close your eyes and visualize a leaf falling from a tree into a slow-moving creek.
- Now, like the leaf, let your breath in and out slowly and peacefully. Inhale deeply and exhale through your nose.
- Repeat twenty times, then gradually let your breath return to normal.
- Finally, take a few moments to sit with your eyes closed and notice the difference in how you feel.

---------------------- ----------------------

To inhale fully is to fill ourselves with the energies of life, to be inspired; to exhale fully is to empty ourselves, to open ourselves to the unknown, to be expired.

— Dennis Lewis

Yogic Breathing...

- 🪷 Boosts your metabolism.
- 🪷 Uses muscles that improve your posture without any additional effort.
- 🪷 Keeps lung tissue supple, allowing you to take in more oxygen.
- 🪷 Tones your abdominal muscles.
- 🪷 Builds up your immune system.
- 🪷 Reduces tension and anxiety.

Furthermore... your nasal passages filter and warm the air, ridding it of dust particles and pollutants.

Allow Yourself a Good Cry

Let's be honest. Crying feels good, so why don't we do it more often? When you're stressed out, time-crunched, financially strapped, or suffering from major hormone fluctuations, give yourself a good release. Don't stifle your sobs. Let them out.

Society might say it's better to smile and suppress your tears in the name of "putting on a good face." But science tells us that it's perfectly normal and healthy to turn on the waterworks to let out your frustrations. Human beings cry for many reasons: to relieve stress, reduce hormone and chemical levels in the body, and help us become calm again.

Just as rain washes away dirt from the streets, tears clear away emotional mud that can clog your ability to continue with your day. Crying is as valuable as sneezing or coughing. So next time you feel that familiar lump entering your throat, excuse yourself and let yourself have a good cry.

There are people who laugh to show their fine teeth, and there are those who cry to show their good hearts.

— Joseph Roux

Classic Tear-Jerker Films Guaranteed to Make You Cry

- Love Story
- Terms of Endearment
- Bambi
- Forrest Gump
- The Color Purple
- Steel Magnolias
- Beaches
- Ghost
- The Way We Were
- Mask
- E.T.
- It's a Wonderful Life
- Cold Mountain
- Stand by Me
- Sophie's Choice
- Old Yeller
- Brian's Song
- Fried Green Tomatoes
- Romeo + Juliet (1996)
- The Notebook

Lose the
Emotional Baggage

Think of how you feel after you've carried a heavy suitcase for a couple of blocks and are finally able to put it down. You're relieved, unburdened, lighter... and happier. When you put aside your emotional baggage — guilt, anxiety, worry — you benefit from the same relief. But those emotions won't leave unless you banish them from your being. The problem is, letting go of emotions and feelings is usually much harder than moving something heavy.

If you truly love yourself and want to take time for yourself, you need to let go of the negativity in your life. It's nearly impossible to relax if you're always carrying around bad feelings. You've got to stop yourself when you start worrying about things you can't change or have no control over... when you fret over how people perceive you and your life... when you blame yourself for other people's problems. Call it tough love. Snuff negative, counterproductive thoughts and feelings the moment they enter your mind... and be kind to yourself every minute of every day.

Be kind to yourself, to others, and everything around you. Beauty becomes an attitude and a way of life.

— Alexandra Stoddard

Let Go of the Past

Let go...
    of guilt; it's okay to make
    the same mistakes again.
Let go...
    of obsessions; they seldom
    turn out the way you planned.
Let go...
    of hate; it's a waste of love.
Let go...
    of blaming others; you are
    responsible for your own destiny.
Let go...
    of fantasies so reality can come true.
Let go...
    of self-pity; someone else may need you.
Let go...
    of wanting; cherish what you have.
Let go...
    of fear; it's a waste of faith.
Let go...
    of despair; change comes from
    acceptance and forgiveness.
Let go...
    of the past; the future is
    here — right now.

                      — Kathleen O'Brien

Just Laugh

When was the last time you laughed? Really laughed?
So hard that your belly hurt and tears streamed down
your cheeks? As we grow older, this type of laughter
just doesn't find its way into our lives as much as it did
when we were children. We have to work harder, but the
benefits are well worth it.

Laughter forces you to just let it all go and think of
nothing at all for a few seconds of time. It can leave
those happy feelings lingering inside you long after the
moment has come to an end. It reduces tension and
creates a relaxing effect for the entire body. Laughter is
a perfectly simple, low-cost way to de-stress and awaken
the carefree child within.

Laughter reminds you that... daily incidents are
unimportant and not worth getting worked up about.
Laughter is God's tranquilizer. Laughter calms the soul and
releases endorphins, which are the feel-good hormones.
Use laughter as your inner therapist.

— Suzanne Somers

Make Yourself Laugh

- Make ridiculous faces in the mirror until you have no choice but to laugh.
- Do a little laughter visualization. Picture your coworkers or classmates dressed in baby bonnets and diapers, or picture all the men dressed in women's clothing and vice versa.
- Only read the comics section of the newspaper. Toss the serious stuff in the recycling bin.
- Go a little overboard with your makeup and paint yourself as a clown for a day. People you know will undoubtedly laugh when they see you, and this will make you laugh as well.
- Buy a joke book.
- Spend a few hours with a small child. That is sure to bring laughter into your day.
- Visit the comedy section at the video store. Rent a bunch of laughs to fill your evening.
- Look at Halloween photos from the past. They'll definitely bring a chuckle of memories your way.
- Surround yourself with funny people who laugh a lot. Laughter is contagious, you know.

Expand Your Mind

You may spend your adult days troubleshooting, problem-solving, and doing other mentally challenging tasks. But what have you learned lately? Have you recently pushed yourself to explore a topic you previously knew little about?

If you're like most people, you spent about twelve years — or more — of your formative years going to school five days a week, nine months of the year. You memorized multiplication tables, recited the preamble to the Constitution, and read Shakespeare. But then you grew up and left behind the chalkboard dust, uncomfortable desks, and rigors of textbook lessons. Sure, it's great not to have homework anymore. But that doesn't mean your mind — and your spirit — wouldn't benefit from taking a class or learning a new skill.

We are creatures of routine. Every day we go through the motions of what we did the day before. Coffee: check. Drive from garage to office parking lot: check. Return phone messages: check. You get the picture... and you can easily envision your own daily schedule of events. Does it sound mind numbing? Wake up your brain. Take a Spanish class, learn to samba, or tackle a crossword puzzle.

Unspeakable joys are showered on us by the exertion of our mental faculties, the quest of ideas, and the tranquil contemplation of knowledge.

— Honoré de Balzac

Mind Games

Learn...
 To play a musical instrument.
 To paint, sculpt, or make pottery.
 Something new: take a course at a college or community center.

Do...
 Crossword puzzles, Sudoku, or jigsaw puzzles.

Join...
 A study group or a book club.

Play...
 Games such as Trivial Pursuit, Scrabble, and Boggle.

Sharpen Your Memory...
 When you learn something new, create a mnemonic device to remember it. For example, the capital of Maine is Augusta. Create a mental snapshot or phrase to help you remember, such as, "A gust of wind blew down Main Street."

Catch Some Z's

So many people deprive themselves of sleep by staying up too late to finish today and getting up too early to get a jump-start on tomorrow. Even though it's nice to feel like you've packed as much as possible into your precious twenty-four hours, it's important to remember that not getting enough z's can make the day a lot less productive and you a lot more grumpy.

Never underestimate the importance of sleep. It is energy for your day, fuel for your fire, and an essential cooldown for your over-exercised brain. After a long, busy day, sinking into a warm, comfy bed can be the greatest pleasure in the world. No matter how intense life gets, making time to get a good night's sleep should never drop to the bottom of your priority list.

When your body cries out for sleep, give yourself as much as you need. Long twelve-hour stretches, if that's what's called for. Put a sleepy message on your voice mail. Let yourself go wherever sleep wants to take you.... Whoever needs desperately to reach you can wait. Give up the coffee and the soda and whatever other energy enhancers you've come to rely on, and reconnect with the sweet, awesome power of natural sleep.

— Rachel Snyder

Sweet Dreams

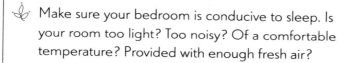 Make sure you have a comfortable bed. A firm mattress and pillow are best.

 Make sure your bedroom is conducive to sleep. Is your room too light? Too noisy? Of a comfortable temperature? Provided with enough fresh air?

Do a relaxation exercise.... Create a time when you can just savor the delicious sensations of your own body in your own space, free from obligations and worry.

Do some light reading....Try to choose a book that you can pick up and put down easily.

Leave your worries outside the bedroom.

Make your last hour before bed as peaceful as possible. Save intense conversations for another hour of the day. Avoid scary or suspenseful movies or TV shows.

Allow yourself to sleep — or, if your body chooses to stay awake, remain calmly mindful of yourself.... Don't try to force or control anything, not even sleep. Just be aware of yourself and your body and let your mind go where it will.

Get up after a half an hour or so, and do something you like or need to do. Decide that since you're giving yourself this waking time, you might as well do something pleasant with it.

— Katherine A. Albert, MD, PhD

STRESS-FREE

So what are the tools we can use to calm our nerves and open our minds? Here comes the good news... we all have the inner resources that are needed: courage, optimism, humility, humor, intuition, acceptance, forgiveness, love, and yes, patience. These inner resources are to our souls what medicine is to our bodies.

— Joan Lunden

Take a Sick Day for the Soul

Think back to those childhood days when faking illness was considered an art form used for one very important purpose: to guarantee a great day of sleeping in, watching TV all day long, being pampered, and wearing your pajamas to breakfast, lunch, *and* dinner. Ahh, the luxury of a (not so) sick day.

Now all it takes is one quick phone call and the day is free for your taking. So why not take advantage of this wonderful way to rejuvenate, relax, and take a break from the usual cycle of life? This mini-vacation will no doubt revive you and boost your spirits, brainpower, and energy for the days to come.

Each person deserves a day away in which no problems are confronted, no solutions searched for. Each of us needs to withdraw from the cares which will not withdraw from us. We need hours of aimless wandering or spates of time sitting on park benches, observing the mysterious world of ants and the canopy of treetops.... A day away acts as a spring tonic. It can dispel rancor, transform indecision, and renew the spirit.

— Maya Angelou

Play Hooky

 Act like a Kindergartener: Wake up early to watch cartoons; stay in your pajamas all day long; eat cookies for breakfast; have naptime; run around outside; eat peanut butter and jelly for lunch; laugh a lot; make a mess; be completely carefree.

 Act like a Teenager: Paint your nails bright red; read magazines and take the quizzes; eat chips and drink sodas; chat on the phone for hours at a time; ride a roller coaster; watch scary movies; read trashy novels; don't call your mother; break all the rules.

 Act like a Responsible Adult: Balance your checkbook; clean the house; make to-do lists; pay the bills; do the laundry; organize the closet; catch up on some reading; buy a gadget for your kitchen; go grocery shopping; eat three well-balanced meals; go to bed early.

Find Refuge at Home

Flopping on the couch and switching on the TV can be as wonderful a comfort to a busy person as a bottle is to a baby. But turning off the TV — and the computer, personal digital assistant, mobile phone, and pager — can be even more relaxing and satisfying for the soul. Once a week — you pick the night — hit the pause button on the DVD player of life and take a spiritual snack break of sorts.

Leave the dishes in the sink, the laundry in the dryer, and the car in the driveway. Unplug yourself from everything except maybe the stereo. Order your favorite takeout dishes or prepare simple finger foods and kick off your shoes.

Spend the time alone, invite friends over, or enjoy an evening of conversation and companionship with your spouse and children. Consider it a weekly retreat without the hassle of traveling to a rustic cabin in the woods. This night is your time to let the events of the week sink in.

I need more time to be still, to think, to develop a deeper relationship with myself. More time for laughing, for loving, and listening to the music I love.

— Susan L. Taylor

You: Unplugged

Treat your living room like...

A Camp Circle:
- Tell ghost stories, sing songs, or tell jokes.
- Make s'mores in your fireplace (or using your stove or microwave).
- Illuminate the room with candles.

A Tropical Beach:
- Make good use of comfortable couches and chairs and recline.
- Consume fruity beverages, and if you can, serve drinks out of coconut shells.
- Stock the stereo CD-changer with island-inspired tunes, such as reggae, steel drum music, or Jimmy Buffett albums.

A Remote Cabin:
- Play board games or cards.
- Stargaze in the backyard.
- Go for an after-dinner walk in the woods.

De-Clutter

We all have clutter. You may choose to refer to this "clutter" by other names, such as memorabilia, collections, hand-me-downs... the list goes on. But the truth is that clutter by any other name is still... clutter.

The excess junk in your life creates an unnecessary amount of chaos. It keeps you from finding things, such as your keys, and causes you to trip over other things, such as piles of books, clothes, or photographs. (Side note: anything in piles is most likely some form of clutter.) Creating more room by ridding yourself of the things you no longer need allows you to reorganize the things you choose to keep. De-cluttering creates an incredible sense of freedom: the freedom to say, "No, I don't need these things in my house," to say, "Yes, I am in control of my life," and to exclaim proudly with pleasure, "Today, I am making a fresh start!"

Simplifying is not necessarily about getting rid of everything we've worked hard for. It's about making wise choices among the things we now have to choose from.... So it's about deciding what is important to us, and gracefully letting go of the things that aren't.

— Elaine St. James

Clean House

🌿 If it breaks your heart to throw things away, make a huge tax-deductible donation to a worthy charity. It will make you feel better knowing you are helping those in need.

🌿 If it is covered in dust, it is time for it to go.

🌿 If its home has been in the back of your closet for the last 365 days, it has overstayed its welcome.

🌿 Say goodbye to anything you refer to as a gadget, doodad, thingamajig, or whozee-whatsit because you don't know its proper name.

🌿 If it belonged to an ex-boyfriend who broke your heart at least two years in the past, burn it.

🌿 For every four pairs of shoes you own, give one pair away.

Clean Out the Closet

One of life's great unsolved questions is why women hold on to clothes that make them feel bad about themselves. Every woman has something (or many things) in her closet that she should toss: that pair of jeans that has never fit right, the expensive, oversized sweater that is beautiful but feels too bulky, anything overly faded and with too many holes — but not in a cool way.

Today, vow to donate every item of clothing that doesn't make you feel attractive. But before you start tossing, take some time to try on everything: every T-shirt, pair of pants, woolly sweater, bra, and special-occasion dress. You'll remember what it was about each item that prompted you to purchase it in the first place. You'll also see wardrobe combinations that maybe weren't obvious given the prior state of your closet! Consider making simple alterations, such as turning a pair of jeans that are too short into a new pair of cut-offs. Along the way, note items that you're missing or would like to buy to complete various outfits so that next time you're shopping, you have a mission. Most importantly, experiment. Be outrageous — nobody's looking!

Clothing is such an easy way to define an image, to help you project whatever it is you want the world to understand about you.

— Heidi Klum

What to Keep, What to Lose

As you comb through your closet, deciding what to toss and what to keep, consider this list of wardrobe staples:

20 Classic Wardrobe Pieces

Tops: Cashmere sweater, sequin top, parka, trench coat, fitted blazer, overcoat, leather jacket.
Bottoms: Menswear trousers, wool A-line skirt.
Outfits: Evening dress, sexy suit.
Feet: Black flats, black pumps, knee boots, strappy evening sandals.
Accessories: Fancy earrings, black leather bag, sequin evening bag, a good watch and leather tote.

Pamper Yourself

Pamper: "to coddle, indulge, spoil... to gratify the wishes of, especially by catering to physical comforts." Pamper is such a wonderful word with an even more wonderful definition, and yet most of us rarely have occasion to say it when talking about how we treat ourselves. Why? Mostly because of the zillion excuses that stand in our way: too much to do at work, too busy at home, low on cash, high on responsibilities — the list goes on.

Pampering yourself should make its way to the top of your priority list at least once or twice a month. Why wait around for someone else to make you feel good when you can do it yourself? You deserve a little extra tender, loving care, and it's up to you to remember that. Pampering yourself is the best way to feel loved, and loving yourself is one of the best and most important stress reducers imaginable. Be the king of your castle, or at least queen for the day, and coddle, indulge, and spoil yourself silly.

Nurture yourself. First, always, yourself. Yes! Give yourself the time, the love, the undivided attention you so often give to others. Sing, dance, read, cook, sew, run, swim, be.

— Rachel Snyder

Learn How to Luxuriate

Prepare
- 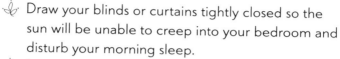 Draw your blinds or curtains tightly closed so the sun will be unable to creep into your bedroom and disturb your morning sleep.
- Set no alarms, external or internal, and completely clear your thoughts before your head hits the pillow.
- Sleep until both your mind and body feel rested, and even then, close your eyes for a little quiet meditation.

Purchase
- Go to the store and spend at least a half-hour in the beauty section. Purchase everything from nail polish to a new robe, or buy yourself a gift certificate in advance to your favorite beauty salon.
- Buy yourself a bouquet of your favorite fresh flowers.
- The mall is an essential stop on your pamper day to-do list. Treat yourself to at least one thing that looks great on you.

Pamper
- Put on your most comfy clothes.
- Light sweet-smelling candles, and turn up your favorite tunes.
- Eat by candlelight in your pajamas.
- Cuddle up in bed to watch your favorite movie.

Fill Your Life with Fragrance

Dish soaps are scented with lemon, laundry detergent is "spring fresh," bedsheets are sprayed with lavender, and clothes closets are paneled with cedar. While you may not think about it, the way things smell makes a difference in just about every aspect of your life.

Aromatherapy takes that concept a step further with the use of essential oils. The aromatic essences are naturally extracted from plants. While the smell of baking cookies might make your stomach growl, a massage coupled with aromatherapy can relieve aching muscles and reduce stress.

The nice thing about essential oils is you can use them anywhere. Spray rosemary essence mixed with water in your office to boost your creativity. Rub a bergamot oil infused lotion on your temples to soothe and calm yourself while waiting for a dentist's appointment. Burn a geranium aromatherapy candle while you're balancing your checkbook to evoke feelings of stability and harmony.

You can close your eyes, cover your ears, refrain from touch, and reject taste, but smell is part of the air we breathe. It's the one sense you can't turn off. We smell with every breath we take, and that's 20,000 times a day.

— Martin Lindstrom

Make Scents

Essential oils are available at health-food and aromatherapy stores and by mail order. Use just a few drops on your pulse points. Look for a mention of the essential oil's Latin (botanical) name, country of origin, or method of extraction on the label, and avoid products advertised as "fragrance oil," "nature identical oil," or "perfume oil."

Here's a basic guide to the benefits of ten popular essential oils:

- Bergamot: Soothes and calms.
- Chamomile: Comforts and restores patience.
- Eucalyptus: Balances and frees the mind.
- Geranium: Evokes feelings of stability and harmony.
- Grapefruit: Revives and eases.
- Jasmine: Stimulates imagination and passion.
- Lavender: Rejuvenates and calms.
- Lemongrass: Cools and calms nerves.
- Peppermint: Revitalizes and instills confidence.
- Rosemary: Increases awareness and creativity.

Room Spray
Blend ten drops of any one of the essential oils above with ½ cup of water and mix well. Pour into a spray bottle with a fine mist setting.

Aromatherapy Perfume
Blend one tablespoon of a carrier oil such as jojoba oil or sweet almond oil, together with 15 to 25 drops of your favorite essential oil. Then transfer to a dark glass bottle or container.

Soak in the Bath

After a long, stressful, not-so-happy, humdrum day, there is nothing more gratifying or soothing than a soak in a warm, bubbly bath. This remedy not only soothes your stiff neck or achy back, but also your heart, mind, and soul.

The solitude experienced in bathing allows time to clear your thoughts and feel at ease. Baths can be both relaxing and therapeutic, awakening your senses and soothing your soul. Let your body become weightless and sink into the warm, soothing water. Let your troubles wash away from you and concentrate on clearing your mind. If adding essential oils to your bath, inhale the scents. Be open to their healing and rejuvenating powers. This is your time to pay special attention to mending and reviving whatever it is in your life, mental or physical, that needs extra comfort and care.

Do not underestimate the blessing of a bath. It can calm your mind, relax your tired, tense body, and soothe your stressed spirit. It can help you drift off to the exquisite relief of sleep or wake you up and help you greet the day with enthusiasm.

— Sarah Ban Breathnach

Stress Buster Bath Blend
    4 drops bergamot essential oil
    4 drops geranium essential oil
    2 drops vetiver essential oil

Mental Re-energizer Bath Blend
    4 drops basil essential oil
    4 drops lemon essential oil
    2 drops rosemary essential oil

Muscle-Soothing Bath Blend
    3 drops black pepper essential oil
    5 drops grapefruit essential oil
    2 drops rosemary essential oil

Add to a very warm bath and disperse well — or blend with 1 tblsp grapeseed oil or 1 tblsp unscented bubble bath and add to a warm bath. Soak in the bath for 15-20 minutes inhaling the vapours. Do not get bath water in your eyes as it will sting.

— Carolyn Selby, PhD

Get Out of the House!

Remember when Mom would command, "Go play!" and send you out of the house for the afternoon? Now as an adult, it's probably hard to believe how tough it is to tear yourself away from the same chores that prompted your mother to send you packing. There's always something that needs to be done: throw in another load of laundry, pay bills, weed the garden. You can't help yourself sometimes.

There are also times when you just need to heed Mom's orders to "Go play!" even if she's not there to tell you. Being at home can be as much (or even more) work than being at work! When you need to relax, take off and really leave behind the pressures of your life. Your escape can be as simple as a walk around the neighborhood. The only requirement is that it can't have anything to do with "work," i.e. household chores or any task you get paid to do.

There's almost always a way to squeeze in a "play break" no matter how harried your schedule may be.

Go outside and try to recapture the happiness within yourself; think of all the beauty in yourself and in everything around you and be happy.

— Anne Frank

Kick Yourself Out!

🌱 Head into the mountains (or your nearest outdoor recreation area) for a hike, or if you're more adventurous, for a backpacking or camping trip with a friend, spouse, significant other, and your dog, if you have one. Exercise, clean air, and bathing in fresh-water lakes will energize you — and leave the bank account intact. Plus, the dirt on your kitchen floor won't seem so shocking after a few days of sleeping on the ground.

🌱 Be a tourist in your hometown. Go to an art museum, stroll the zoo, take a historic homes tour, bicycle through a neighborhood filled with architecturally interesting houses, or sit on a bench in a public place and people watch.

🌱 Start taking a nightly after-dinner walk.

🌱 Make a weekly coffee-shop date with yourself. Take an hour (or longer!) to sketch, write, read, or chip away at a project you've been longing to do but never seem to have the time for.

Go Away for a Girls' Weekend

You and your group of pals may have pondered this idea of going away for a "girls' weekend" before... or maybe you've already made it an annual tradition. Among your peers, you know how good it feels to let it all hang out... to be the girl you were before you left your parents' house for your own... to be the woman you've grown into, but without the trappings of adult responsibilities.

A girls' weekend is a special time to indulge. Dress up or dress down. Get a manicure and pedicure... and maybe a massage, too. Watch as many chick flicks as you want. Listen to your favorite sappy songs and sing along at the top of your lungs. Stay up late and sleep in. Dance. And laugh till it hurts.

It's up to you and your friends to decide how to spend the time. Just be sure to put some distance between you and your domestic and professional responsibilities.

It's important to have as much fun as possible while we're here. It balances out the times when the minefield of life explodes.

— Jimmy Buffett

Girly Getaways

Go... Big

 Splurge for a spa weekend or yoga retreat in a destination you've been dying to experience.

 Put on your most-fashionable walking shoes, and hit the shops of Rodeo Drive, the Magnificent Mile, or Fifth Avenue.

 Spring for a guided tour (gourmet meals included!) of an outdoor destination — bicycling through Napa Valley, kayaking the Baja Peninsula, backpacking in the Rocky Mountains... or somewhere more exotic!

Go... Mid-Range

 Book a weekend in Las Vegas. Enjoy buffets galore, nightclubs, shows, an outrageous amount of neon, and gambling.

 Plan an all-day, all-night extravaganza... right out your front door. Organize a spa day at a local salon. Then lunch like ladies at a white-tablecloth establishment. Retire to a hotel to have a pajama party.

Go... Small

 Go car camping with your pals at a nearby nature preserve, national forest, or park. Get dirty, roast marshmallows, hike, and gab.

 Have an old-fashioned slumber party! Clear your house — or at least a part of your house — of spouse and children. Order pizza, make popcorn, play music, watch movies, and stay up all night playing games and talking.

Ask for Help

So many women take on more than anyone would ever expect of them. One of the best ways to make time for yourself is simply to ask for help when you need it. If you're overwhelmed at work, let your boss know you need help. The next time a friend offers to baby-sit or help with your gardening, say yes. Your friend will feel good about helping you, and you'll truly appreciate that break.

Everyone needs a hand every now and then. People don't offer their time without considering the possibility that you might say yes. They probably also consider that if you do accept their offer, you might help them with something in the future. Face it: finishing an arduous task in half the time thanks to a second pair of hands feels great. If you open up yourself to the possibility of having help, not only will you save time, you'll most likely find your friendships strengthened through the shared experiences.

You *can't* do it all. And even more important: YOU DO NOT *HAVE* TO DO IT ALL.

— Maria Shriver

Share the Pain

- Organize a house-painting (or other not-so-fun job) party. You provide the pizza, refreshments, and "favor" coupons redeemable for a reciprocal task.

- At your workplace, divide projects into three piles: urgent, long-term, and delegate. Get to know your office's eager beaver and mentor him or her. If you're still at the eager beaver stage, buddy up with a coworker to share work before upcoming vacations, dueling deadlines, and other instances when you're simply overwhelmed.

- Don't undermine yourself by taking on more than you can realistically accomplish. Call a maid service if a long-lost friend or a relative announces an unexpected stay at your house and there's no way you can clean before he or she arrives. Order groceries to be delivered, too, so you'll have a nice selection of snacks waiting for you and your guest when you arrive home to your clean house!

- Be a good planner and communicator. Always look ahead on your calendar to see what conflicts might arise in your work and home lives.

Take a Minute

Have you ever wondered who invented the modern work week? It just doesn't seem fair to work five days and receive only two days of respite... and even then it's hard to call the shopping, household chores, and other activities of a typical weekend a real break.

For every hour you're awake, take a 60-second break, every day. Set your watch to remind you every hour to go to a quiet place where you can stand or sit, breathe deeply, and allow your mind to wander to thoughts that relax you. After a minute has passed, go back to what you were doing before. You will feel more relaxed and energized. Consider it a quick charge for your mental batteries!

Take the short escapes to another level: 60 minutes per day of alone time, 60 hours a year for a personal retreat, and 600 hours of vacation time annually... but why not start with the hourly micro-vacations? That priceless one-minute escape will provide a quick getaway — and no one will think twice about your short absences.

If you sit down to meditate, even for a moment, it will be time for non-doing. It is very important not to think that this non-doing is synonymous with doing nothing. They couldn't be more different.

— Jon Kabat-Zinn

Take 60

Relax Any Time, Anywhere: A short "let go" relaxation is a nice transition from the busyness of your day. Sit tall in a chair or on a firm pillow cross-legged on the floor. Close your eyes, feel where the eyelids touch... Watch your breath for a few moments... take your time... on your next exhale, open the mouth and sigh, a nice long haaaaaa. Imagine any little cares, concerns and worries of the day being emptied from your good friend, the brain. Imagine them in waves washing over your skin like warm water from the shower, then swirling down the drain. Repeat two or three times.

Neck Tilt and Shoulder Shrug: The "weight of the world" is often carried in the neck and shoulders. I love these stretches and can feel shoulder and neck tension release immediately. Do in regular clothing, anytime, anywhere, such as an hourly break from the computer.

 Neck Tilt: Sit tall, shoulders down from ears. Slowly tilt your head to the right side. Rather than bringing your ear to shoulder, consciously extend and lengthen your neck into the space right above your shoulder... Pause... Pull left shoulder down. Hold for 2-8 breaths... Return to center. Feel the sensations within the neck. Repeat on opposite side, holding for two or three enjoyable breaths.

 Shoulder Shrugs: Sitting tall, inhale; shrug your shoulders up under your ears. Squeeze... Hold... now release shoulders with a "let-go" sigh. Again, shrug shoulders up, feel the muscle squeeze... hold the tension... now, release with a let-go sigh. This time really mean it! Roll shoulders forward in a slow circle and back in the opposite direction — two to three times. Take your time, repeat all the above, then pause... eyes closed. Observe the sensations within the neck and shoulders.

— Lilias Folan

Be an Early Bird

Get up an hour before you absolutely have to. Yes, this sounds painful and wrong. But the morning (or afternoon, if you work nights) is so peaceful simply because you have it all to yourself. The house is quiet; the streets are empty. You can go for an energizing jog, read the newspaper, drink tea without interruption, and reduce your typical mad rush to a slow shuffle.

Changing one's schedule is never a snap. Once you get into the groove, it's easier to look forward to your special morning routine. Picture yourself beginning your workday wrapped in a fluffy terrycloth robe, your feet cushioned in soft slippers, and your hand cradling a warm mug filled with something aromatic and caffeinated. Ahhh.

The extra time will help you mentally organize your day long before you get to the office. You'll begin your day refreshed, relaxed, and with eyes so bright and fresh people will wonder what you're doing differently.

We're all working with the same amount of hours; it's what you do with those hours that makes all the difference.

— Mary Lou Retton

Catch the Worm

🌱 Stay in bed even though you're awake. Enjoy the comfort of your bed. Stretch, meditate, or write in your journal, chronicling your dreams from the night before or random thoughts of the morning.

🌱 Train yourself to wake up without an alarm clock by going to bed a little earlier than normal and telling yourself each night the time at which you wish to wake. If this would never work for you, consider investing in an alarm clock that can awaken you with a gradual increase in volume using music from a favorite CD, chimes, or other serene sounds.

🌱 Trade your morning shower for a bath. Light candles, burn incense, listen to relaxing music. Spend extra time on your beauty routine. Pluck your eyebrows, do a mud mask, air dry your hair, slather on the moisturizer.

🌱 Before getting dressed, read the entire newspaper or a chapter of a good book.

🌱 Water your houseplants or stroll through your garden.

Multitask No More

Multitasking seems so efficient. You return phone calls while driving the kids to soccer practice. You balance your checkbook while scarfing a tuna sandwich over your lunch hour. You squeeze in a workout at the gym — but you bring work to read while pedaling on the exercise bike. Unfortunately, the perception that multitasking saves time is often not the reality. Juggling tasks often takes more time than doing them one at a time. There are interruptions, you lose focus, you drop one project midstream to deal with other pressing matters.

Instead of rushing through your to-do list, tackling two and three things at a time, slow down. Prioritize. Focus on the job at hand and complete it before moving on to the next thing. You will still accomplish what you need to, but you won't feel nearly as rushed. The quality of your work will most likely improve, as will your sense of pride in everything you do.

If you take one problem at a time, one solution at a time, one step at a time, you can handle anything.

— Martina Navratilova

Slow Down

By trying to be
everywhere at once
I am nowhere
By trying to be everything to
    too many
I am no one

Most of us after having
spent many years
working to live

Spend many more years
living to work

And when finally
there is no more work
We don't know how to live

— Natasha Josefowitz

Just Say No

Chances are you've been asked to do something you didn't want to do or didn't really have time to do — organize a school fundraiser, knock on doors to raise awareness and money for a political cause, or host a book club meeting. But you still said, "Sure, no problem!"

It's hard to let down friends, neighbors, coworkers, and others who rely on you. But without boundaries, you invite others, and their priorities, to take over your life. Next time someone asks you to "help out," seriously consider what you'll be giving up to fulfill the obligation. You obviously want to give back — otherwise you wouldn't be so overextended! So make sure you're offering your skills and services in the areas that are most meaningful to you.

And don't be afraid to take shortcuts. Pick up a gift card instead of shopping for a handpicked birthday present. Suggest a bookstore café as an alternative to hosting the book club at your home. Be deliberate in how you use your time — and learn to push aside the guilt that comes with saying, "no." You'll be happier for it.

We need to distinguish between selfishness and self-care. A no to one thing is a yes to something else.

— Joan Borysenko

Say "No" in the Politest Possible Way

🌱 I'm sorry, I won't be able to.
🌱 I wish I could, but I'm busy that day.
🌱 I've got plans... I've got a previous engagement...
I've got an appointment I can't break.
🌱 Maybe next time.

Buy Time

🌱 Let me check with my husband/partner/spouse.
🌱 I need to look at my calendar.
🌱 I need to think about it; I'll get back to you.
🌱 I might have to work.

Have a Policy

🌱 I'm sorry, I have a policy: I don't help friends move...
I don't lend people money... I don't dog sit.

Love It or Leave It

So much of what you do in this life is preparation for the future. You get an education to get a job. You get a job to build a life for yourself and your family, piece by piece. You forgo sugary desserts today so you can fit into a slinky dress tomorrow. You're always working toward something that has yet to be.

If you see today's labor as a sacrifice for tomorrow, consider this: the average worker will spend 80,000 hours of her lifetime on the job. That adds up to nine consecutive years, if you were to work twenty-four hours a day, seven days a week. The point is: if you don't enjoy what you do for a living, you're cheating yourself.

Few people can afford to quit their jobs, but if you know that what you're doing now isn't what you'd like to do for the rest of your working life, it's time to start working on an exit strategy. Change is never easy... you might need to go back to school, take a lower-paying, entry-level job, or save a pile of cash to get started on your dream career path. The payoff, however, will be priceless. You'll be buying back your life.

What makes me sane makes me successful, and what makes me successful makes me sane.

— Bonnie St. John

Create Your Escape Plan

Do...

 Explore all the options. Your career might not be the problem. Maybe it's your boss, management, or current position that isn't right for you. Is it time to start looking for a new employer, not a new career?

 Find a mentor: someone to confide in, someone who will encourage you, give you advice, and keep you on the path toward your goal.

 Seek career counseling. Given the potential cost of a career change — especially if you're considering going back to school — this is a wise investment. A counselor is an unbiased person who can help you truly assess what potential career paths might best suit your lifestyle, personality, and skill set. Books on the topic also will provide helpful tips.

 Gain experience in your new career field. Volunteer or find a part-time job in the area that interests you. If this is something you can do while still working at your current job, even better.

Don't...

 Rush into anything. Seriously weigh the pros and cons and all the possible effects of a career or job change.

 Limit yourself to career fields for which you already have skills. Consider your interests.

 Worry if you second-guess yourself. It's only natural to have those feelings.

Visualize Yourself Doing What You Want

In your mind's eye anything is possible. That's why so many successful people say they like to visualize themselves achieving a goal. Olympians envision themselves completing a gold medal-winning performance; business leaders imagine themselves closing a big deal; politicians picture themselves winning the next election. The practice instills confidence. You can actually see yourself doing the thing that excites you, and in the process, you become comfortable with yourself in a new role.

Taking time for yourself can be as simple as taking a few moments each day to form a mental picture of yourself doing that thing that you so badly want to do. The dream won't magically come true. You've got to do the work to make it a reality. But part of getting there involves mentally preparing yourself for your shining moment. What will you do when you finally make it to your final destination?

To create prosperity, we need to visualize ourselves living as we desire to live, doing what we love, feeling satisfied with what we attain, in a context of other people doing the same.

— Shakti Gawain

Paint a Mental Picture

🌱 Make visualization a morning ritual. Before you eat breakfast, go through the motions in your mind. For instance, what would it be like to ask your boss for a raise today? Envision the big event of your day before it happens.

🌱 Keep a visualization journal. You already mentally place yourself in all kinds of situations. Who hasn't imagined how they might react if they won the lottery! As human beings, we can't help but picture how different scenarios might work out. Put that ability to work for you, and let your gut reaction to your visualizations guide you.

🌱 Reinforce visualization with positive self-talk. You can nab that business deal, you can resolve a conflict between yourself and a friend, and you can cook healthful meals for yourself. Don't undermine yourself with negative "I can't" thoughts.

Face Your Fears

Fear is such a natural, instinctive feeling. It's scary to be alone in the dark... to jump off the high-dive at the local swimming pool... to go to a party where you don't know anyone. But some fears come from a place that can't be explained. Logic doesn't register. You feel safe in a car, but not in an airplane. Catching a common cold doesn't worry you, but the remote possibility of contracting Avian flu has you in a panic. Your friend's 14-year-old dog is as gentle and harmless as a stuffed toy, yet you don't want to get too close to it.

Improving your life and taking time for yourself can mean working on the things that sometimes hold you back from realizing your dreams. Fears and phobias can be conquered. There are many methods: therapy, hypnosis, desensitization, anxiety medication. The biggest step is to seek help. Make the leap necessary to start working past what's holding you back.

Avoiding danger is no safer in the long run than outright exposure. Life is either a daring adventure or nothing.

— Helen Keller

Strong Women

Strong women are those who know the road ahead will be strewn with obstacles, but they will choose to walk it because it's the right one for them.

Strong women are those who make mistakes, who admit to them, learn from those failures, and then use that knowledge.

Strong women are easily hurt, but they still extend their hearts and hands, knowing the risk and accepting the pain when it comes.

Strong women are sometimes beat down by life, but they still stand back up and step forward again.

Strong women are afraid. They face the fear and move ahead to the future as uncertain as it can be.

Strong women are not those who succeed the first time. They're the ones who fail time and again, but still keep trying until they succeed.

Strong women face the daily trials of life, sometimes with a tear, but always with their heads high as the new day dawns.

— Brenda Hager

Make Money Your Friend

Money, money, money. Just the sound of the word can cause comfort, excitement, or anxiety. It's difficult not to want new clothes, a nicer vehicle, a bigger house, and it's easy (thanks to easy credit!) to convince yourself that your future paychecks will keep up with your expensive tastes today. Such a drive to "have it all" causes many women to both love and hate their bank accounts — and to dream about inheriting a windfall.

For all its allure, money's impact in people's lives may not be as great as it appears. Many psychological studies show that the super rich are no happier or more fulfilled than people with middle-class incomes. Think of your finances like your health. Everyone overindulges every now and then, but you feel and look so much better when you eat right and exercise regularly. Spend within your means, put money aside "just in case," and budget for those luxuries you'd rather not live without. Money is power... but only when your balance sheet is in the black.

You'll have more than enough when you realize that you can be rich at any income because you are more than your money, you are more than your job or title, than the car you drive or the clothing you wear.

— Suze Orman

Spend for You

Create a Budget
 You know what your fixed costs are: housing, utilities, transportation, groceries, health care, clothing. Once you've covered the essentials, you can spend (or save) the rest of your earnings however you like.

Trim the Fat
 Realistic spending is a lot like realistic dieting. Forgo a can of soda and save 100 calories. If you get a haircut every eight weeks, start going every nine weeks and you will save the cost of one haircut every year.

Keep Tabs
 Debit and credit cards have turned overspending into a sport. Regularly balance your bank accounts.

Think Before You Buy
 Thoughtful shopping is good for your bottom line. Buy the $100 pants if you know you'll wear them for years to come. Don't buy five pairs of $20 pants you're not so sure about, because they could end up stuffed in the back of your closet.

Get Rid of the Guilt
 There's nothing personal about money, but so many of us attach feelings to how we — and the people in our lives — spend and earn money. It's important that we control our dollars, not the other way around.

Be Deliberate

When you picked up this book, you made a decision. You decided you want to take more time for yourself. But for you to get any benefit out of these pages, you also need to examine the thousands of little choices you make every day. It's up to you whether you take a luxurious bubble bath scented with lavender or a quick shower... whether you eat a healthful lunch or look to the nearest vending machine for sustenance... whether you feel relaxed and refreshed when you wake up in the morning or stressed and harried.

Today and every day, be deliberate. Would you feel better about yourself if you watched TV for an hour after dinner or went for a long walk with your dog?

You may feel like a bad day gives you license to binge on junk food or break your commitment to quit smoking. Instead, try to lift yourself out of a foul mood with positive actions — take a nap, watch a funny movie, call a good friend, make a funny face in the mirror.

Always ask yourself: will this decision improve the quality of my life? When forces out of your control threaten to ruin your day, don't forget: it's up to you how to react.

— E. D. Frances

Decisions, Decisions, Decisions

In an Ideal World...

- Where would you live?
- What schooling would you have completed?
- How much would you earn?
- How much money would you have saved for the future?
- What clothes would you wear?
- How physically fit would you be?
- What foods would you eat for breakfast, lunch, and dinner?
- How would you spend your days?
- What would your love life be like?
- What would you do for a living?
- What would you do for spiritual fulfillment?
- Who would be your friends?
- What kind of friend (sister, wife, daughter) would you be?

Now the most important question: what decisions can you make to turn these ideals into reality?

Take Time for Every Dream

It's so important to have dreams... to have something you are working toward at all times. Those dreams can be as small as finishing the book you've been reading for a month or as big as making a career change or moving to a new city. Not every goal you set will be attained, but if you set a variety of goals, the ones that you do achieve will bring a great feeling of satisfaction, and the ones that don't... well, they will just keep you reaching for more.

Remember that taking time for your dreams means taking time for you. Nurture and ground yourself. Try to find satisfaction in everything you do. Stop rushing around — it doesn't get you anywhere. Truly think through your actions, and always aim for the targets that keep your wheels turning and you moving forward. Live the life that will make you happiest... every moment of every day.

Setting goals is one of the most powerful ways to create the life you really want. People with goals succeed because they know where they are going.

— Joan Lunden

Each day
I will remember...

I have choices
that I can take care
of myself
and that it can be
my first choice.

That it is okay
to say no whenever
necessary
to stand up for myself,
then let it go!

That I do not
have to please others
or be everything
to everyone.
I do not have to be it all...
who I am now
is enough.

I can be honest
and still be kind,
set boundaries
and stick to them.
I can consider my own needs.

I will remember
to honor myself,
that it is my responsibility
and divine right to do so...
each day.

— Pam Reinke

ACKNOWLEDGMENTS

We gratefully acknowledge the permission granted by the following authors, publishers, and authors' representatives to reprint poems or excerpts from their publications.

Doubleday, a division of Random House, Inc., for "You must have a room..." from THE POWER OF MYTH by Joseph Campbell with Bill Moyers. Copyright © 1988 by Apostrophe S Productions, Inc. and Alfred van der Marck Editions. All rights reserved. And for "Be kind to yourself, to others..." from DARING TO BE YOURSELF by Alexandra Stoddard. Copyright © 1990 by Alexandra Stoddard. All rights reserved.

Karen York for "It is simply gratifying to nurture something..." from "Grow Better, Feel Better, Live Longer," published by gardenforever.com. Copyright © 2003 by Karen York. All rights reserved.

Sterling Publishing Co., Inc., New York, NY, for "Let color in and she will..." from APRIL CORNELL DECORATING WITH COLOR by April Cornell. Copyright © 2004 by April Cornell, a Sterling/Chapelle Book. All rights reserved.

Mitchell Beazley, an imprint of Octopus Publishing Group Limited, for "Red is the color of..." from COLOUR HEALING HOME by Catherine Cumming. Copyright © 2000 by Octopus Publishing Group Limited. All rights reserved.

W. W. Norton & Company, Inc., for "The woman who needs to create..." from MRS. STEVENS HEARS THE MERMAIDS SINGING by May Sarton. Copyright © 1965 by May Sarton. All rights reserved.

Shambhala Publications, Inc., for "When you write, don't say..." from WRITING DOWN THE BONES by Natalie Goldberg. Copyright © 1986 by Natalie Goldberg. All rights reserved.

HarperCollins Publishers for "Most of us have been trained..." from THE BEST YEAR OF YOUR LIFE by Debbie Ford. Copyright © 2004 by Debbie Ford. All rights reserved. And for "Solitude is taking pride in..." from QUIRKYALONE by Sasha Cagen. Copyright © 2003 by Sasha Cagen. All rights reserved.

Margaret Cho for "Sometimes when we are generous...." Copyright © 2004 by Margaret Cho. All rights reserved.

Grove/Atlantic, Inc., for "Friends are like home..." from THE ART AND POWER OF BEING A LADY by Noelle Cleary and Dini von Mueffling. Copyright © 2001 by Noelle Cleary and Dini von Mueffling. All rights reserved.

Alpha Books, a division of Penguin Group (USA), Inc., for "When you do something wonderful..." from THE COMPLETE IDIOT'S GUIDE TO ASSERTIVENESS by Jeff Davidson. Copyright © 1997 by Jeff Davidson. All rights reserved.

Rodale, Inc., for "If we treat our bodies properly..." and "If you take one problem..." from SHAPE YOURSELF by Martina Navratilova. Copyright © 2006 by Martina Navratilova. All rights reserved.

Simon & Schuster, Inc., for "I find the best antidote..." from HOW TO STOP WORRYING AND START LIVING by Dale Carnegie. Copyright © 1944, 1945, 1946, 1947, 1948 by Dale Carnegie. All rights reserved. And for "Make sure you have a comfortable bed" from GET A GOOD NIGHT'S SLEEP by Katherine A. Albert, MD, PhD. Copyright © 1996 by Elizabeth A. Ryan. Abridged with permission of Simon & Schuster Adult Publishing Group. All rights reserved. And for "What makes me sane..." from SUCCEEDING SANE by Bonnie St. John. Copyright © 1998 by Bonnie St. John. All rights reserved.

Hamlyn, a division of Octopus Publishing Group Limited for "Because time is the one thing..." and "The Fruit and Vegetable Fast" from NEW AGAIN! by Anna Selby. Copyright © 1999 by Octopus Publishing Group Limited. All rights reserved.

Henry Holt and Company for "Many people ignore the profound effects..." and "Eat a breakfast that includes..." from FOOD AND MOOD by Elizabeth Somer, MA, RD. Copyright © 1995 by Elizabeth Somer. All rights reserved.

Chronicle Books for "Habits are often formed because..." from THE MERIT BADGE HANDBOOK FOR GROWN-UP GIRLS by Cherry Pedrick. Copyright © 2005 by Herter Studio LLC. All rights reserved.

Rodmell Press for "To inhale fully is to fill ourselves..." from THE TAO OF NATURAL BREATHING by Dennis Lewis. Copyright © 1997, 2006 by Dennis Lewis. All rights reserved.

Kathleen O'Brien for "Let Go of the Past." Copyright © 2007 by Kathleen O'Brien. All rights reserved.

Crown Publishers, a division of Random House, Inc., for "Laughter reminds you..." from 365 WAYS TO CHANGE YOUR LIFE by Suzanne Somers. Copyright © 1999 by Suzanne Somers. All rights reserved. And for "Clothing is such an easy way..." from HEIDI KLUM'S BODY OF KNOWLEDGE by Heidi Klum and with Alexandra Postman. Copyright © 2004 by Heidi Klum Company LLC. All rights reserved. And for "You'll have more than enough..." from THE 9 STEPS TO FINANCIAL FREEDOM by Suze Orman. Copyright © 1997 by Suze Orman. All rights reserved.

McGraw-Hill for "When your body cries out..." and "Nurture yourself" from 365 WORDS OF WELL-BEING FOR WOMEN by Rachel Snyder. Copyright © 1997 by Rachel Snyder. All rights reserved. And for "So what are the tools we can use..." and "Setting goals is one of the most..." from WAKE-UP CALLS by Joan Lunden. Copyright © 2001 by New Life Entertainment, Inc. All rights reserved.

The Free Press, a division of Simon & Schuster Adult Publishing Group, for "You can close your eyes..." from BRAND SENSE by Martin Lindstrom. Copyright © 2005 by Martin Lindstrom. All rights reserved.

Random House, Inc., and Little, Brown Book Group Ltd. for "Each person deserves..." from WOULDN'T TAKE NOTHING FOR MY JOURNEY NOW by Maya Angelou. Copyright © 1993 by Maya Angelou. All rights reserved.

Essence for "I need more time to be still..." from "A Quiet Talk with Myself" by Susan L. Taylor (Essence: 23.n6, October 1992). Copyright © 1992 by Essence Communications, Inc. Copyright © 2004 by Gale Group. All rights reserved.

Hyperion for "Simplifying is not necessarily about..." from LIVING THE SIMPLE LIFE by Elaine St. James. Copyright © 1996 by Elaine St. James. Reprinted by permission. All rights reserved. And for "If you sit down to meditate..." from WHEREVER YOU GO, THERE YOU ARE by Jon Kabat-Zinn. Copyright © 1994 by Jon Kabat-Zinn. Reprinted by permission. All rights reserved.

Warner Books, Inc., for "Do not underestimate the blessing..." from SIMPLE ABUNDANCE by Sarah Ban Breathnach. Copyright © 1995 by Sarah Ban Breathnach. Reprinted by permission of Warner Books, Inc. All rights reserved. And for "You can't do it all" from TEN THINGS I WISH I'D KNOWN BEFORE I WENT OUT INTO THE REAL WORLD by Maria Shriver. Copyright © 2000 by Maria Shriver. Reprinted by permission of Warner Books, Inc. All rights reserved.

Dr. Carolyn Selby, www.therapyessence.com, for "Stress-Buster Bath Blend." Copyright © 2006 by Dr. Carolyn Selby. All rights reserved.

Doubleday, a division of Random House, Inc., and Penguin Group UK for "Go outside and try to..." from THE DIARY OF A YOUNG GIRL: THE DEFINITIVE EDITION by Anne Frank. Otto H. Frank and Mirjam Pressler, Editors, translated by Susan Massotty. Copyright © 1995 by Doubleday, a division of Random House, Inc. All rights reserved.

Random House, Inc., for "It's important to have as much..." from A PIRATE LOOKS AT FIFTY by Jimmy Buffett. Copyright © 1998 by Jimmy Buffet. End Paper Maps. Copyright © 1998 by Anita Karl and Jack Kemp. All rights reserved.

Lilias Folan for "Relax Any Time, Anywhere" from THE BIG BOOK OF RELAXATION. Copyright © by Lilias Folan. All rights reserved.

Broadway Books, a division of Random House, Inc., for "We're all working with the same..." from MARY LOU RETTON'S GATEWAY TO HAPPINESS by Mary Lou Retton. Copyright © 2000 by MLR Entertainment Inc., and Momentum Partners, Inc. All rights reserved.

Natasha Josefowitz for "Slow Down" from TOO WISE TO WANT TO BE YOUNG AGAIN. Copyright © 1995 by Natasha Josefowitz. All rights reserved.

Hay House, Inc., Carlsbad, CA, for "We need to distinguish..." from INNER PEACE FOR BUSY PEOPLE by Joan Borysenko, PhD. Copyright © 2001 by Joan Borysenko. All rights reserved.

New World Library, Novato, CA, www.newworldlibrary.com, for "To create prosperity..." from CREATIVE VISUALIZATION by Shakti Gawain. Copyright © 1978, 1995, 2002 by Shakti Gawain. All rights reserved.

Pam Reinke for "Each day I will remember...." Copyright © 2007 by Pam Reinke. All rights reserved.

A careful effort has been made to trace the ownership of selections used in this anthology in order to obtain permission to reprint copyrighted material and give proper credit to the copyright owners. If any error or omission has occurred, it is completely inadvertent, and we would like to make corrections in future editions provided that written notification is made to the publisher:

BLUE MOUNTAIN ARTS, INC., P.O. Box 4549, Boulder, Colorado 80306.